the stages of falling

maddie ceasar

CONTENTS

to the ones who stuck by me throughout this journey of adolescence. to my beautiful family who has shown me love and acceptance when i needed it most. to my lovely friends who have supported me with everything i do. to the ones who never stop dreaming with their hearts

falling for you

standing next to you
i can actually breathe,
we can take on the world
and live out our dreams.
a place for just
you and me,
where we can both be ourselves,
and we will finally
be happy.

-she is my love and you can't change that

your openness and empathy
towards my struggles
and ability to broaden
your mind about
my identity
means more than you
could ever comprehend.

-*thank you*

the words go through my head like the water that
poured down the river we use to sit near and have
picnics at every summer. you use to reach for my
hand and we would pray for the days moments. for
the bountiful amounts of sunshine and food. for the
breeze that carried laughter all around our tiny
bodies. what tiny bodies in a world full of greater
forces and concepts. the sun once warmed my scalp
like the day you exclaimed you loved me. a sudden
giddy feeling of the world being on myside, our
side. she wraps her arm around my shoulder and
tells me it's going to be alright. my insides flutter
and dance like the grass we plucked from the
ground and tied in knots.

-summer love

the stages of falling

hundreds of miles away
your hand is on mine.
hundreds of miles away
our fingers intertwined.

hundreds of miles away
i gaze into your eyes.
hundreds of miles away
we stare at the infinite sky.

hundreds of miles away
our heartbeats connect.
hundreds of miles away
your gracefulness projects.

hundreds of miles away
your soul shines.
hundreds of miles away
courage flees from your spine.

hundreds of miles away
and you still have my heart.
hundreds of miles away
yet we are not apart.

-*distance won't defeat us*

she will never know
how anytime she
speaks
my heart
grows
with each word
and flutters
with every beat.

-you fuel my life

but what i couldn't get out of my mind
was the taste of her warm dark lips,
sweet sugary honey,
the feeling of her arms wrapped around mine

       –how safe and at home i felt,
          in her arms.

  perhaps after all this repentance,
i truly discovered what the faults
in their views of love were.
if this is what love actually is meant to be,
     what i had found was much stronger.

-she is the definition of love

how deep;
your words dripping
down my spine,
encasing every inch
of my body.
a feeling of warmth,
a feeling of home,
a feeling of *you.*

-*you are my comfort*

the stages of falling

she is the moon
and the sun
and the stars
and the galaxy.
she is my entire
world and
she is my whole
universe.
life would not
exist without her.

-mother nature

i wish i could see the sun rise
on the pink sand and grasp the
palm of my lovers hand.
i wish i could look into her dark
blue eyes and realize that everything
is going to be alright.
that the days will soon pass by and by
and the nights where demons
use to creep will no longer continue
to disrupt our sleep.
all of the tears that we once wept
will soon be full of laughter and dreams—
one that we will no longer
have to memorize in order for them to
play in front of our eyes.
they are no longer the crisp,
elongated verses we sang to ourselves
that spit utter lies.
we will stand next to one another alive,
our hearts full of
that sun rise on the sand,
palm in palm,
hand in hand.

-*in our dreams*

Let's hold hands and run away together. I know you are afraid of the consequences, of what will come when you reveal the scars of your heart to a world full of knives

One heart combined, we will tackle the spears that are thrown at us. We will dodge every spike and dagger aimed towards our love.

Vagabonds from each city that denounces our souls, we will continue to search for a place to call home.

Eagerly awaiting the day our raw and battered beings are welcomed into open arms.

-our definition of love

goosebumps arise as
you look into my eyes.
the words
i love you
seem to harmonize.
floating from
our bodies
all the way
towards the sky.

-angels dancing

each phrase that slithers off of your
tongue is intoxicating,
every sentence leaves me craving more and
more,
the butterflies begin to crawl in my stomach and my
body feels buzzed,
warm and giddy.

—however consuming a substantial amount of your
treacherous speech
leaves my mind
uncontrollable and cloudy
while the world spins
until my vision turns

black.

*-did you know it is possible to get drunk off of
someone's words?*

falling out of love

why do we constantly
dance around the
important questions
like moving checkers on the board
trying to run away
from the things
that matter most.

-never ending games

the words pour out of you
like waves crashing
against the cold rough sand,
forceful and striking hard at
the surface,
however,
the water
slowly penetrates deep below and
settles within,
forever present.

- your words i can't forget

a piece of my heart
hangs inside the place
where you and i shared
our first embrace.

-they told me to move on but a slice of my heart
will always be with you

nothing hurts more
than a perfectly formulated
lie, and
how did i know?
—there was a
small hanging piece of thread
that slowly unraveled
creating an unmistakable
hole in your words.

-you said you loved me

you do not deserve to see
how my eyes light up like
the moon on a
clear black night.

you do not deserve to trace
the palm of my hand
and be let into all of the experiences i have had
on this land.

you do not deserve to see
how my stomach rolls
and crashes like
the waves in the ocean
when i tilt my head back
in laughter and emotion.

you do not deserve all of the verses
i hold in my heart
for it is my life you
chose not to be a part.

-you took me for granted

the stages of falling

every time you look
at him my heart

    s h a t t e r s

    into fragments of broken
memories and dreams,
    pieces so agonizing
      one move could
        s e v e r
        any inch of me.

-you left me for him

you parade into my life
as if your past words
had never sliced my heart
open with a knife.

-the wounds don't heal

i need to understand that
the words i say mean
nothing to you
yet i can't seem
to comprehend
that the conversations
we use to share
are all dust too.

-i don't want to forget

i was your sponge.
i was always there
to clean your act up when
you were a mess.
i soaked in all
of your negativity.
i did all of
the work you didn't
want to put up with.
i let you use me
over
and
over
and
over
again until one day,
you soaked up all
of my offerings,
and then
abandoned me to
dry.

-i am used up

the stages of falling

i have not heard from you in weeks and i am
worried about what i did to make you upset this
time.

i miss the warmth of my skin as we touch and you
melt away all of my sorrows and sins.
i miss your bright smile and your golden kiss.
i miss the way my stomach explodes into butterflies
with every word from yours lips.
i miss the vibrant colors that flash in front of my
eyes when i wake up next to your hips.
i miss the days when you would make the darkness
of the universe leave me be.
without you here, my world is gray and the sky
seems so empty.

  —i guess i was foolish to assume you would
come back after
    the moon took your place,
     i was foolish to take for granted our last
      goodnight embrace,
       and
     i was naive to believe i would always see
        your face.

-oh sun, please come back

i just wanted
to call you mine
but you never came
when i left the door
open wide.

-*why didn't you come?*

where am i to go
when you were the only
home i had known.

-i am lost without you

i try to forget
but the smell
of your perfume
lingers in my room.
i don't want to
admit it but
i think i still
i miss you.

-holding a piece of you

the stages of falling

i vaguely remember that summer night
laying with you in mid-july.
here we thought our hearts
ran connected like the
constellations in the sky.
infinite stars and possibilities
of what we could do
when i was yours
and you were mine.
your palm in my hand
as i stared into your glassy eyes.
laying here felt as if
there was no existence of time,
just us and the chills of love
crawling up and down our spines.
maybe we were naïve to believe
the sun would no longer rise
in order for our love
to last a lifetime.

-one last night with you

each word is like a
tack in the body,
a shooting pain making
its way straight into
the heart.
glass shattering with
every syllable,
the pieces of sentences
burrow themselves
under the breaking skin.
the phrases spoken
fill up the lungs
like water,
gasping for air,
but unable to find anything
left.

-suffocating in the thought of you

the stages of falling

they knew what scenes we put out into
the open, so naive and childish,
tragedy would soon close off the final act.

i never expected the crowd to erupt with
roaring cries, my composure strong and steady,
yet you were unable to take the criticism.

tears streamed down your face as you
ran across the stage.
none other than i was left,
attempting to pick up the broken pieces of
the show.

as the reviews were posted,
you took back your word and plastered my image as
your defense.
i took the fall,
leading me on a desolate journey,
one of which i was my only companion.

my one question to you,

did it feel just like a play?

how can you
still tell me you
love me,
when you
ripped my life to
pieces with no
apology.

-i am still waiting

the stages of falling

each time my eyes
gaze up to the reflected glass,
the image before me screams back
all of the words that fell from your mouth.

-*your words have sunk into my blood*

how can my heart
decay with abandonment
from something that was
never mine in the first place.

-grasping onto thin air

the stages of falling

your mouth
danced around
mine,
tracing
every step i made,
pulling me in
and out to the music
of our souls.
sometimes when your
heart was in the music,
you accidentally
stepped on my foot,
but that only made me
want to dance with
you more.
when the music cut off,
the pure taste of sugar
was left in my mouth.
later as i crashed,
i craved you more and more,
but you were nowhere to be found.

-never kiss and tell

you latch on to anyone
who can bring you a sense
of belonging,

and then

> once the feeling of
> being the center of attention
> runs stale,
> you unhook yourself

and scope out a
> fresh set of

eyes

of which

you can be
the new focal point of.

-*you jump around from one person to the next*

if i meant
that much to you,
why did you
go and break
my heart in two?

-questions that will never be answered

one day i took scissors to
the gaudy, sticky gum in my hair
which day after day,
consumed each bit of me.
while chopping it away
got rid of you,
it left a noticeable hole
in the way i carried
myself.

-losing a part of me and you

you lured me in with your inscrutable statements, like a book with no title on the outside, leaving me with the utter curiosity of what was hiding beneath your skin, you knew that i was naïve and credulous. you took advantage of the way i laid my heart out to the world. you knew i gave you the benefit of the doubt, which must have been the go ahead to manipulate my brain. you knew that i shared every inch of my thoughts with you, only to have them ripped to shreds and shared with the world. i unwrapped my skin revealing my darkest fears only to have you make them a reality. i no longer know what information is mine, and what has been wrongfully stolen from me. were you making a list of every insecurity i had when i was with you? it is like you were crossing out each item with every word you said. you exploited my heart, you controlled my mind, and yet i am still the one that is the fool?

-a requiem to you

2:47 am and
once again,

my mind is playing
fantasies of what we could be
if we were
more than friends.

-*visions that will never become a reality*

a drawing of us is tucked away between the wooden
slates of my bed frame.
maybe in there it will be safe,
away from all of the broken memories
and the heart break
and pain.
maybe one day i can look at it
without feeling disdain,
without feeling contempt for how you chose her
over me,
how you crushed my entire world
leaving only debris.
maybe one day i can pull
the drawing out from under my bed
and finally get the memory of you
out of my head.

-but that day is not today

the stars connect and form constellations
that spell out your name,
so excuse me for looking up to the
black void and constantly being
reminded of all the pain.

-everywhere i go i see you

pencils are tapping and erasers are smudging

but all i can think about is the day you asked me to work on math problems with you. the equations bounced between us as you tried to figure out why the relationship would not balance out. yes, it looked so easy when you first thought about the numbers being together, but it did not go as planned. we tried so hard to make it work, but you cannot change the numbers to be something they are not.

the clock on the wall is ticking through my body

just like my heart when you said we needed to talk. i know that we have been moving in circles trying to catch up to one another like the hands on the wall. it is about time we ran out of energy.

the bell rings and chairs are pushes across the floor

but i am still sitting here with your words screeching in my ears. i have not figured out the equations on my sheet of paper. my heart is still beating through my chest. i stare at my name on the paper, one that will never fall from your lips again. i hand in my test and all of the memories that went with it.

-test anxieties

i know it well,

all of the i love you's
and the assuring i will never leave's,
the back and forth texting
and the butterflies and bees.
the eternal conversations
and the midnight calls,
days of constantly seeing each other
and the tearing down of our walls.
exposing all of our darkest secrets
and sharing our nights,
feeling like we will be together
for the rest of our life.

but one day you will decide that this is not enough,
you will make the decision not to stay,
for even though it is words of forever you use
to trust,
it is inevitable that things will change.

-in the end it is just me

the stages of falling

i sometimes struggle with math but i do not need to be a mathematician to equate that while i thought the equation was

me+you,

the entire time you were using

you+you,

and there was never a me. i do not know how i mixed up the two equations?
science perplexes me but i do not need to be a scientist to clearly understand that my hypothesis

"if she tells me she loves me, she is speaking the truth,"

was proven false. all of my observations were thrown off by the night you decided i wasn't good enough for you.
english comes easiest to me, yet i will never comprehend how our romance story turned into a tragedy. i will never be able to grasp the hidden meaning behind your **"i love you"** and **"i will never leave."** i will never digest why you decided to skip all of our rising and falling actions, and head straight to the resolution. most of all, i will never fathom what on earth your character's intentions were, and why you brought me into your washed up story in the first place,

-there are plenty of things i do not understand, but what i do know is that i am too good for you

45

was it
foolish to assume
that maybe you
loved me too?

-questions that will never be answered pt. ii

the stages of falling

i don't know what to say
to make you want to stay.

i don't know how to make you
pick up the phone
and not speak the words
where i end up alone.

i don't know
who you've become
and why our love
has turned numb.

i don't know what to do
to stop our hearts from
breaking into two.

-why does it always end like this

they say that winter symbolizes death in literature,

but oh how they failed to explain the lurch of the
subzero winds
        spreading across my entire body, the ice that
      collects under my eyes where the tears once fell
      down my face, the stinging burn of the air that i
        cannot seem to catch, the phrases you spoke
    pouring from the clouds, the sky a blanket of gray
             that follows me every way i turn,

                they say that winter
                symbolizes death in
                literature,
          and i have found that you are
           winter in my book.

-thankfully the seasons change

if you cared
that much about me,
why did you leave?

-*"it's not you, it's me"*

you played
me like a movie,
knowing
the ending
before the
opening credits
ever began.

-bad intentions

it's late at night and the placid wall is stained with the scraps of tape and the bright blue sticky tack that once strung together the pieces of my life that all use to trace back to you. the fragments of memories collect under my broken finger nails, my fingertips drenched blue and stained with the lies that fell from your mouth. my walls are bare and i don't know if i can stand the idea of our existence vanishing into thin air. i dig my nails into the wall but it is no use. you have engraved your existence into my skin, and never returned to the room that i am trapped in.

-pictures of you are scattered across my bedroom floor

we were phobos and deimos,
mars' moons,
chasing after one another in circles
around the one concept we vowed to
never let go.

*-but we could never reach each other, the orbit was
too strong.*

no matter what i try to do,
my heart keeps crawling
back to you.

-but we will never be together

a heavy pendulum
swings back and forth
inside my cage of
bones.
a heart pressing against
the cracks,
pressure spreading
from my head to toes.
each memory
increases the weights
pace,
pushing my heart
further to the edge.
the bones crack under pressure,
spilling thoughts of you into
my blood stream.
a sickeningly sweet high
of our love
soon sweeps me away in
the undertow.

-an overdose of you

a picture of me and you
hangs ripped in two,
a piece of lint covered tape
placed over the crack in the photo
but the damage is something
one can't undo.

*-you tore apart my heart and tried to fix it with "i
still love you"*

maddie ceasar

falling to the ground

the silence was shattered
by your words.
they echoed throughout
the air
and bounced
off of the walls that were
collapsing.

you took
my heart
right out of my body,
throwing it out into
a world of hate,
bloody and all.
you stole
the words that i
laid perfectly
in between the bones
of my spines,

the ones i locked away
until it felt safe
to bring out again.
you swiped them
from me like a bandit
as if it were a game,
and while
you obtained the answer,
my life came crashing
to the ground.

you lift
me naked in
front of the room,
exposing every
inch of my mind
and inner thoughts.

-what gave you the right to share my story?

too many countless
nights were spent
wishing away
the parts of me
that should have
stayed.

-stolen pieces

some nights the thoughts
creep back into my
bones and bury themselves
deep inside.
i feel remorse and ache
spread and take over
my brain.
why do i blame myself
for such pain others
inflicted upon me?
is it the fact that i was
once told not to
shed a tear and to get
over it, let it be?
however, it was you,
not me, who presented
the tools to push me
in too deep.
how is it fair that i
continuously carry the
weight of deceit.

-broken therapy sessions

dare not let
the words slip
through the cracks
of my teeth,
for they may
see the real me
and decide to leave.

-repressed feelings

i wish i could run until
i reached the end of the
ocean we use to
think would lead us
to the celestial bodies
in the sky.
i wish i could climb the
clouds the way we imagined,
stairs to a place that
is not full of monsters
and never ending disaster.
i wish the moon was actually
smiling back at me and
as we drove around the land,
she was truly following me
to make sure i was safe.
i wish my veins were
actually blue,
we use to think that
they were pumping color
and creativity throughout
our bodies.
i wish the stars were
actually ours,
we would name them and
feel like we had a
place in this scary world.

-but then we grew up

they carved their existence
into my skin
yet i swore i would never
let them win.

-bruised bones

my skin turns inside out and
my hands are burning like
gasoline set to flame and
my heart feels like the
weight of the world is crashing
down and my feet feel like
they are sinking in quick sand
and i am unable to catch my
breathe as it's running a marathon
and tears stream down my eyes
like the flow of a river
and my insides do flips into a
pool of sorrow and guilt.

-why can't i like boys that way

staring blankly at my phone
trying to obtain
happiness through
nonexistent likes held
captive in a screen.

-social media and the cycle

living your truth
is like wearing
your heart on the
outside of your chest,
caught in between
trying to protect it
from the nails
of others that try
to rip it apart,
and burying it under
your clothes
desperately trying
to hide what makes you
you.

*-wanting to be inside and outside of those closet
doors*

a stained alarm clock
ticks on the
bedside,
its hands spiraling
        endlessly.

cups stack up on
the bedside,
your half lit
cigarette lays
lifeless—
drowned out by the musty
water.
window shades
collect
fragments
of our memories
all dust,
have not been touched in
a
century.

the wallpaper is
lifting off
the walls,
your fist fell
through the
paper thin surface
as
did your sanity.

the lampshade
is shattered
on the ground near
the door,
it took one
accident
to shatter
the stability
of the sturdy.

my heart
is starting
to peel
like the wallpaper,
maybe if i
would have moved
out of this
bed
i could have
    saved

        her.

*-i never got to tell you about the
butterflies in my chest.*

three letters yet it seems,
that no matter how much
i try to be me
you will constantly
erase my identity.

-you tell me i can't be gay

you touched my body
as if it was your
property,
your make shift home
for the moment,
and you had no concerns.
you broke in and out and
left the door wide open.
people watching your act,
yet the only words
spoken were
"why did you wear that?"

-as if a dress was consent

maybe it's the way the fire sputtered when you said his name.

maybe it's the way your head jutted out when i said the word gay.

maybe it's the way you etched death into the human race.

maybe it's the way your eyes gleamed of ignorance and hate interlaced.

maybe it's the way your voice thundered as the sky rained down.

maybe it's the way you constantly kicked me on the ground.

maybe it's the way you dish out slurs like a baseball game.

maybe it's the way you have never tried to change.

-yet you still don't understand why we are no longer friends

your voice brings back the subtle bangs of thunder every time it rains/ the rain drips down the window pane as your words manifest inside my brain/ i don't know if you realize what you say and how it causes the earth to sway /every word that comes out of your mouth adds to the never ending swirling clouds of pain/ each time you repeat your past mistakes the pace picks up and trust is taken away/

-the good things about storms is that they always pass

my mind is a mirror
distorting every
compliment i get
into a twisted
empty gesture.

-low self esteem

the stages of falling

how can i
write about
happy things
when i piece
together
words from
the memories
hidden deep
within the
cracks of my
bones

—i think that i have
found out,
grief is the
only home i know.

-i have learned to find comfort in discomfort

my body is stained,
your words carved
and branded into
every crevice and
inch of my skin.
any time my eyes
see the marks
i'm flooded with
the memories that
once were a reality.
mascara from
years past lay
smudged beneath my
sunken eyes.
no matter how much
friction i apply to the skin
the memories won't ever
fade away.

-the damage is permanent

the stages of falling

she speaks the words
of cherry blossoms
on the pink trees,
slowly blooming
into an immaculate
fruit,
one that forever
attracts the eyes
of each stranger
who passes by.

-they don't pick her, therefore she does not see her
beauty

i thought for once i
wouldn't be put last,
but that figment of
imagination quickly
passed.

-prioritization

did you think i wouldn't notice the foot prints
collecting on my body? i wouldn't see my skin
wearing down and fraying from being worn out so
much? that i wouldn't notice the dirt you smeared
across my image? did you think that i would
continue to let you use me as friction to collect all
of your dirt and pain? was it really reasonable to
assume that my hard surface would never crack?

-you treated me like a door mat

avert your eyes from the reflection in the mirror,
let the water run so the fog covers your tears.
take a finger and trace out the perfect silhouette,
get rid of stomach rolls and curves but you'll never
be perfect.
go from a double-d to a b,
but your mind and the mirror will never agree.
smooth out the stretch marks on your hips and
thighs,
but that won't change your lips
being the wrong size.
fix every detail that isn't correct,
erase the mistakes until there is nothing left.

-body issues

trying to gain the
ability to feel emotions
after being numb for so long
is like trying to revive a
heart that flat lined months ago.

-recovery

i so desperately
crave the feeling of
ripping out the bad
memories i intricately
tucked away between
the spaces in the middle
of each one of my ribs,
but if i tear them out,
how can i deal with
emptiness and never
ending voids within
my bones?

-*where do i begin?*

what if i've upset the moon: anxiety vs. clarity

please calm down the sky won't always be this dark/ I DRAINED THE LIGHT OUT OF THE SKY, I RUINED EVERYTHING ONCE AGAIN/ you need to eat, love, your hands are shaking/ IT FEELS LIKE THE WAVES ARE CRASHING WITHIN ME, NOTHING WILL TAKE THIS FEELING AWAY SO WHY SHOULD I BOTHER?/ the world will soon slow down/ IT FEELS LIKE THE WORLD IS SPINNING AND I CAN NOT CONTROL ANYTHING/ the moon will come out again, it's just a cloudy night/ I FORGOT TO TALK TO HER LAST NIGHT SHE MUST BE MAD AT ME, I MEAN, I DON'T BLAME HER/ you need to get sleep, stop worrying about the moon/ HOW CAN I STOP THINKING ABOUT ALL OF THE MISTAKES I HAVE MADE, I NEVER DO ANYTHING RIGHT/shut your eyes, tomorrow is a new day/ IT IS PAST MIDNIGHT, TODAY IS ALREADY HAPPENING/ the moon will show up tonight then, i promise you/ WHAT IF SHE DOESN'T, WHAT WILL HAPPEN THEN?/she will show up, when has she not come back?

it's 3:01 am.
the dull taste of metal has been
absorbed on the buds of my tongue
from the night before.
the clang of the spoon vibrating
against my teeth continues to ring
like the alarm clock that should have
been waking me up in exactly 3 hours.
the futile pills chased down
with the thick syrup
has left a bitter after taste.
my throat has been glued together
and my numerous attempts of
speaking are pointless.
there is nothing to say.
i stare up at the darkness
which seems to stretch far
beyond the galaxies above.
my body is weighed down by
the force of gravity but my head
is spiraling in the vast void.
the knife that was gnawing into
my brain last night has not
stopped cutting and continues to
perforate deeper within my skull.
each second leaves more and
more of my brain deteriorating and numb.
time no longer exists,
only the faint sound of counting to 10
as i try to breathe.
it is 3:02 am.

i just want to know why you think it is okay to try to knock me down to the ground repeatedly.

will you ever let the damn past go. please, continue to steal everything that was once mine and leave me just organs and bones.

rip my skin to pieces, take the clothes off of my back, ransack what i use to call home.

hear my bones clang onto the ground and form a mound of dust and blood and thoughts muddled together. you swing and kick at my body, in attempts to take possession of my soul, yet the bones are a cage to the one part of me you will never be able to graze.

no matter how hard you try, you would never be able to carry the weight of my heart.

-you will not take my heart

we are constantly reminded that any speck or dot on our face is the equivalent to dirt, however i have learned to look at my skin and see the connecting dots as constellations lighting up the world around me.

we are shut down almost immediately for having "too grown up" opinions, yet our childhoods are being viciously stolen away from us as we learn to run in diagonal lines and locate the nearest exists anytime we enter a building.

we are told that in order to be loved we must have the perfect hour glass shape,
however my body is a piece of art that is molded into an imperfect perfection, i am not the product of a machine.

we are force fed the idea of fitting in from the time we step foot on this earth, however not one person's exact genetic makeup and mind are the same, so how can we all confine to an expectation that is virtually impossible.

-broken concepts

vivid recollections of nightmares haunt my reality. the events of the past nights show play throughout my head. unable to grasp the concept of fact or fiction my brain fights itself to no end. the shadows of last night's dream follow me around. every step i make reminds me of the tossing and turning, the sweat pouring down my helpless body. shrinking down my body becomes smaller and smaller until the darkness of my unconscious fears swallows me into another night of restlessness.

-pain entry no. 998

the assortment of miscellaneous bottles are scattered across my night stand. some are half empty, filled with broken dreams that were never fulfilled by the futile tablets. others are depleted and its contents that used to be pills of hope ended up fruitless once again.

each bottle marks the beginning of a new cycle, filled with consequences that reach the darkest depths of the inferno.

it starts with the optimism and naivety of a young child, willing to try whatever you ask of them in return for a reward.
next comes following the requests asked of you. placing the colorful candy into your mouth, you swallow a gulp of optimism.

then comes the aftermath. the devastation of a natural disaster inside your body occurs. waves crash against your stomach sending ripples of nausea. fires wage a war ripping through your throat like the trees. tornadoes spiral down to the ground, tossing about your ability to make clear of any thoughts. earthquakes squeeze and compress the inside of your brain against your skull, explosions bound to happen at any second.

like any kind of grief, you feel numb from all you have lost in the catastrophe that has taken a toll on your life. as you continue to consume the pills, you question if it is really worth dealing with added anguish.
you have two choices; continue to burn your body down to the ground, or to pick yourself back up and begin the cycle once again.

-the cycle of chronic pain

my heart is breaking. innocent children in preschools are no longer just playing hide and seek. they are being taught how to duck and cover, how to try and save themselves from the bullets flying in the air.

there is no such thing as a childhood.

my heart is shattering. the elementary school children are in math class. they are calculating the time they would have in order to escape from an intruder who entered the front of the building.

addition has turned into counting the number of lives that have been taken this year.

my heart is in pieces. high schoolers walk into school no longer fearful of what grade they get on their math exam. they wonder if they will ever get to take it.

no longer worried about the SATS but whether they will be alive to go to college.

my heart is crushed. stepping into a place of worship, the bells no longer chime even though it is time for the ceremony to start. they are replaced with the echoing of gun shots and cries in the air.

we aren't safe where we should be most comfortable.

my heart is torn apart. sitting at a restaurant they peer around the room. they don't search for their waiter coming with food, but for the person who could dish up bullets.

the plate won't protect your life.

my heart is destroyed. people stepping foot outside of their homes into the light of day being flooded with the darkness of whether they will see the light again.

the sun doesn't stay up forever.

my heart is devastated. thousands of innocent lives that can never be revived with the hollow solution of thoughts and prayers.

the darkness fills up my lungs as another wretched night will be spent letting the blistering thoughts bombard my already moribund body. all i crave is to shut out the world, but how can you close out the negative space around you that contains the air you need to breathe?

my heavy eyelids shut but recollections of memories blast through the only place there was once serenity and silence. paralyzed with the fight of needing sleep between my brain and body, the words of others continue to fire in my brain as i lay powerless. evocative images of agonizing events play like i am sitting in the front row of a movie theater, viewing a screening of my traumatic experiences on repeat.

my arms and legs are weighed down by the expectations of others that scream in my mind. so desperately i try to escape, yet the thought of never being good enough acts like a chain around my body. no longer able to move, i pray that sleep will soon wash away the purgatory.

-please let me fall asleep

do you think she forgot about us?/ no moon, you always seem to overthink things/ *but she hasn't come out to talk to us in days*/ so maybe she is going through something rough right now and wants to be alone/ *but what if she just doesn't want to talk to us anymore?*/ i mean,/ *you and i both know she graduated last night. you and i both saw how happy she looked. without us. what if her childhood is over*/but we were there moon.. we were watching over her like usual/ *sun, what if she doesn't come back?*/ she looks up at the sky every day and night, we will always be a part of her universe.

-conversations between the sun and moon pt. 2

8:55 pm/ when you left

my bony feet slammed against the pavement with all the weight of the day i knew you were leaving me. i started to run to stop my toes from the raw ground but the burning traveled through every bone in my body. 206 piercing pains connected like a circuit, spiraling in my blood and burying itself in the veins of my heart. I ran to stop the pain but the bitter and heavy presence of grief in the air stopped the oxygen from reaching my lungs. no amount of stamina and strength could overcome the emptiness of your departure.

9:06 pm/ searching for you

after my legs gave out, i laid on the sturdy pavement bracing myself to find your star. maybe they said you went to heaven but i needed to know that you were here with me in the present. so many lights filled the sky that i did not know where to find you. my eyes frantically searched but the clouds spread across where you were once sitting. my body caved in on itself, for the oxygen still was cut off from my body. if i could not see you then there was no way you could reach me.

9:20 pm/ drifting to you

my eyes flash back to the nights you use visit. i remember you sitting next to me in the eves of terror and distressing dreams. the air that was once biting turned to warmth and comfort filling up my lungs. as you embraced me my bones glued themselves back together. i was whole again. you would sit with me until my body was cohered into a cycle of serenity.

9:48 pm/ not a goodbye

a gentle breeze brushed across my face and my mind was brought back into the present. the cold air still stung but you were there. you had to be. my mind was centered and the clouds disappeared. maybe there were trillions of stars and galaxies up above, but you had to have found a way to follow me. you always were fighting for the ones you loved most.

-minutes pass by as i think of you

falling in love with
myself

you asked me if i was
taking a boy to prom,
as if my long hair
and the clothes i wear
and my press on nails
are an indicator of
an attraction to males.

-i guess you've got me wrong

my life is more
valuable than your comfort.
i will no longer dictate every
move i make in order to satisfy
your taste.
there is nothing wrong with the
way in love i take
but there is in fact something
incorrect about your hate
and how i let your
opinions act as an
enormous weight
upon me.
there is a major error
in the way i pushed
every right of being
a human aside
for your sake.
i will release my
truth out into
the sky until
my vocal chords strain
they almost break.
i will finally live
my life authentically
and **YOU** will be seen
as the disgrace.

-i am gay and you can't change that

they ask how i can know
for sure i like girls
as if it is a question up for debate
like you would choose this life
just to experience the hate and
the pressure and the pain
to know that you saying the word
gay could come out like
the shatter of a plate, like your
words set off a contraption
that dropped a life crushing weight
sending everyone into a panic state
as if you would willingly
throw yourself into a pond of fish
as live bait
to think you would want to feel
like your thoughts are boxed tightly
into a crate just waiting for the
day that you can make a
grand escape but are stuck in a
wretched stalemate.
they ask how i can know
for sure i like girls,
and although it causes pain,
i look them deep in the eyes and say
the same exact way you know
you are straight.

*-don't tell me i'm too young to know, don't say i
don't look gay, and don't you ever dare tell me to
change*

i will not forget the damage
you caused and the pain
you yielded my heart,
but i will no longer let it
define me or how i
live my life.

i will not forget your actions,
but i will forget how you
turned me against myself.

i will be free.

ever since i was little i would look up to the moon
and the crevices on her sunken face would wrinkle
up a bit in the middle. the folds of skin formed a
grin as she beamed her gold down on my forehead
to my chin. i would look into her eyes and pray that
everything would soon be alright, and every
evening she would look down on me and say,

i am here child, look
you made it through another day.

tonight ten years later i wondered if she would still
be my savior. my opal eyes reached the midnight
sky, and she focused in on me as if to say hi. we
may have not talked in awhile, but she gave me that
same old smile. i chanted out

oh moon, when will my life ever be in tune.

she beamed her rays upon my ghostly skin, and
boomed

keep holding on little one,
for life will all make sense soon.

-conversations with the moon

it's absolutely frigid, 24 degrees to be exact, however there are hundreds of places around the world experiencing weather that is far below that 24 degrees which you claimed inadequate. actually, in Antarctica today it is 12 degrees below 0, and in Tugoncani, Russia, walking out doors would lead you to a whopping -20.2 degrees. while you claim to be sick from the cold weather, individuals are outside in the subzero air working twice as hard as you. while you think of the number 24 as unlucky and unbearable, others see it as a blessing and the winning number of the lottery. instead of viewing the number 24 as 24 short steps away from that dreaded 0, start realizing that you are 24 long steps above it, 24 steps— and maybe even more, higher than the others around you.

-perspective is important

your words
were spit
like gasoline into
an open pit of fire.
the flames were
a natural disaster,
spreading rapidly
through our entire
town.

you picked everyone
up with your power
of ignorance,
in the attempts to
burn me down.

the stages of falling

you tried to
erase my entire
identity into only the
slightest bit of
black ash,
containing every
piece of me and
attempting to bury
it in the ground.

little did you know
that water can
extinguish
even the strongest,
most resistant flames.
little did you know
that i blocked out all of the
oxygen,
diminishing your hate.

-i am the water

your wings may be
fragile and broken
but who is to say
they can't gather
the strength to
piece themselves
back together
again.

no matter
what others believe to be true,
just know that we will
continue fighting for you.

-we are all human beings, treat everyone
accordingly

she was told that her
complicated personality
and strong willingness
equated to being
incapable of love

however she soon
found out
those qualities were
actually quite lovable
and it was people's
opinions that she
must learn to overcome.

no statement or decree
will let you control
my body.

-land of the brave and free includes me

your crackled hands are stained with inner creativity. nails each distinct in their shape and tint, formed by the scrupulous effort you put out into the world. the lines on your palms idiosyncratic, experiences and hardships traced into your skin.

opaque cobalt roots hold your body in its central state. as light shines through your rejuvenated skin, the strength of the roots can be seen.

your adamant shoulders stand robust in their beliefs, unable to be amended. your collar bones are hills, slightly above the ground that part to reveal the sun in between.

the stars on your face create depth and captivate one to look at the sky. your emerald eyes hold the pathway to a flourishing garden deep inside of your mind.

your soft rose lips bring out a pop of color in your personality. the hook at the end of your nose draws people in to your artistry.

-i am my first love

you are more than
the hate they say
and the ink
they try to
engrave in your name.

soon flowers will
arise from
my ribs
my love
i am growing.

-i am capable of love

sometimes you have
to pour all of your love
back into the roots
where it first grew.
it is not greedy
nor egocentric for
you to take care
of you.

be the person you have
always wanted to be,
and remember that loving
yourself and others
is key.

maybe one day
you will choose to
open the shutters
of the window
and finally
see the
true potential
that is right
in front of you.

-no one can define me.

i am thankful

for the gray skies and the sun that may never appear
for the ability to breathe in the cold air
for the nights that i don't know if i can keep going
for the quiet drives where you don't know what to
say
for the customers who ask me never ending
questions
for the one who critiques my every move
for the girl who broke my heart into thousands of
pieces
for the flashes of painstaking memories i don't want
to remember
for the pain that sets my body a blaze
for the evenings filled with loneliness and thoughts
for the sleepless nights of self-doubt
for the tears that sting my eyes
for the mascara stains on my pillow case
for the boy who harassed me every day
for the words screamed at me that night of the
bonfire
for the gut wrenching slurs of hate
for the heartless sabotage committed by someone i
loved

for being alive.

the stages of falling

i. your heart is strong, but it is simply impossible for you to carry all of that weight by yourself.

ii. lean on others and ask for their support. iii. it is okay to not be okay all of the time.

iv. you had your first real crush.

v. please don't beat yourself up for loving someone of the same sex.

vi. cherish those feelings of butterflies every time she texts you.

vii. and you also had your first heart break, know that it was inevitable and there was no way things could work out at the time.

viii. you are not unlovable.

ix. please show your body kindness and respect.

x. i understand it doesn't seem like your body is treating you right but it is keeping you alive and letting you experience the wonders of life.

xi. you lost people in your life but you will meet others.

xii. do not wallow in your mistakes and grow from them, move on.

xiii. some days you need to slow down and give your body a rest; as much as it irks you, a car goes nowhere when it is out of fuel.

xiv. others words do not define you.

xv. instead of focusing on them focus on loving yourself for what you're worth (hint, you're worth the galaxy).

xvi. tell others you love them as much as you can because you never know when time is up.

xvii. let loose, laugh loud, appreciate the small things, fall head over heels, because life only happens once.

-eighteen, and still learning

the open waters reflect
an image of hope in
what's to come

Made in the USA
Middletown, DE
09 January 2020

82904101R00076